Malvern M

at

The Abbey

(Malvern Priory Gatehouse)

By

Pamela Hurle

Malvern Museum
at
The Abbey Gateway
(Malvern Priory Gatehouse)

Malvern Museum is housed in one of the town's oldest buildings - the so-called Abbey Gateway. It is usually said to date from the late 15th century, though traces of an earlier building have been discovered in the foundation walls. The building has been quite heavily restored and altered, especially in Victorian times.

The gateway formed the main entrance into the property owned by the monks of Great Malvern Priory, founded in 1085. It is possible that there were other entrances, though no evidence for this suggestion now exists. Its position in a wilderness made Malvern an ideal spot for Aldwin and his followers to set up a monastery, because the monastic life was one of religious devotion that required constant prayer and seclusion from the world. Malvern remained remote throughout the Middle Ages and continued to be obscure and insignificant for a further 300 years after the 16th century dissolution of all English monasteries. It was not until the 19th century that the water cure attracted fashionable visitors and turned Malvern into a popular spa.

In medieval times all visitors to the monastery had to declare their business at the gatehouse which was incorporated into the boundary wall that ensured privacy for the monks and their estate. The monks, following the Rule drawn up in the 6th century by St. Benedict of Nursia, pursued their life of prayer and work behind the wall which separated them and their property from people living in the tiny village of Malvern. The doorkeeper would keep watch through the 'squint' - a small rectangular window let into the thick stonework of the west wall of the passageway under the arch.

When Henry VIII forced the closure of the priory in 1539 as part of his scheme to abolish all monastic life in England, the monks were dispersed, their property disposed of and most of the monastic buildings were destroyed. In Malvern the destruction of monastic buildings was particularly unfortunate because much splendid refurbishment had occurred as recently as the end of the 15th century. The monastic establishment was in prime condition, the most beautiful structure being the church itself with its glorious stained glass, superb encaustic tiles and skilfully carved misericord seats.

By the mid-19th century only three of the monastic buildings remained - a timber framed guesten hall designed to accommodate visitors to the monastery, the church and the gatehouse.

The guesten hall was demolished in the middle of the 19th century because it stood in the way of William Archer's plans for his new Abbey Hotel, which replaced the old Abbey House. At the time few people cared much for the old hall, long used as a barn, but its loss has been much lamented since then. Fortunately fragments of its timber survived and may be seen in the museum.

Turner's 1832 picture showing a lightning strike

The monastic church still stands, of course, and is today popularly known as 'the Priory'. In fact, a priory was not merely a place of worship but the whole complex of monastic buildings including the living quarters and grounds where the monks spent their lives. Their church, purchased by the people of Malvern, became the parish church and it is more correct to call it Malvern Priory Church. The Abbey Gateway has been still more a victim of imprecise use of language. Great Malvern Priory never achieved the independent status of an abbey, being always subject to the supervision of Westminster Abbey; and the gateway had living accommodation for the gatekeeper, so the structure should be called the Priory Gatehouse.

When Malvern Priory was dissolved surviving monastic buildings fell into lay hands. At first the crown leased out the gatehouse and then it was sold, first to William Pynnocke in 1544 and then, a year later, to John Knotsford, whose daughter, Anne, married into the Savage family. Through her the gatehouse became part of the Savage family's extensive estates for over 200 years. Its use and history during this time are far from clear, though probably the 16th century was the period when the most significant alterations were made to it. These included extending the building several feet outwards on the south side. Architect Arthur Troyte Griffith, who knew the gatehouse intimately, suggested in 1940 that the original south wall may have been timbered, like the guesten hall, and ran along the line of the ancient gateposts, which can still be seen. This would suggest that the original building was only about two-thirds of its present depth. The new south wall was then partially faced with bricks. In 1774 the Savages sold the gatehouse to one of Malvern's largest landowners - the Mason family.

In the middle of the 19th century some repairs were carried out and there seems to have been a close connection with William Archer of the Abbey Hotel, whose initials were incorporated into the ironwork. A more major restoration took place in 1891, by which time Miss Palmer of Abbotsfield in Abbey Road had owned the gatehouse for about twenty years.

Unfortunately, evidence that lay in the structure itself and would have shed light on it history has been destroyed by successive building work. Numerous old prints, mostly depicting the north side, enable us to trace some of the changes made over the centuries. But the conclusions to be drawn from them can be only tentative: many artists and engraver tried to present a pretty picture rather than an accurate drawing of the subject.

Henry Lamb of the Royal Library (now Barclays Bank) published many prints of Malvern in the 19th century. His picture of the Priory Church and Abbey Boarding House also shows the south side of the gatehouse.

One of the oldest prints (1731) showing its north side was the work of the brothers Samuel and Nathaniel Buck. They entitled it Malvern Magna Abby (Great Malvern Abbey) thus encouraging a possibly already existing practice of claiming for Malvern's humble little priory the status of a fully independent abbey. They also included some strategically placed trees and a ruined wall next to a remarkably intact gatehouse, all illustrating the temptations that beset the engraver. One wonders how realistic was their perfect set of gates restricting passage through the archway, but they drew the gates in a position consistent with the ancient gate posts.

An early 19th century print shows the boundary wall to the east of the gatehouse in a quite different position from the 1731 print. The 19th century print may well, however, be unreliable. Engraved by Stewart and Burnett, it came from a drawing by G. Shepard 'after a sketch by Mrs. Lathbury' - clearly there was ample opportunity for artistic licence here. By this time a kind of dove-cote shown in 1731 and in a print by Sparrow in 1787 seems to have disappeared - though it does appear in an undated early 19th century print by J. Bradley.

The Buck brothers' portrayal of the north side in 1731

Sparrow's 1787 view

This dove-cote (if it was a dove-cote) is a reminder of the need to exercise caution in using prints as evidence of the history of a building. Each version of the dove-cote is different, the only point of agreement being its actual position at the south west end of the building. By the mid-19th century the dove-cote disappeared and a central weather vane appeared instead. Various external changes were made and the building re-roofed.

Stewart and Burnett's early 19th century engraving.

Bradley's early 19th century print showing the dove-cote at the south west, the same position but a different design from that in the Bucks' picture. Details of the windows and stone-work also differ.

In 1891 the north side, said to be in a dangerous condition because bits of stone were falling into the road, was refaced. At the top a new battlement considerably altered its appearance. Two rooms were added at the west end, and the interior was so much altered that its original plan is now impossible to envisage. Local historian Dr. Charles F. Grindrod was shocked by the 1891 'vandalistic effacement' and considered Malvern to have lost the old gatehouse as effectively as it had earlier lost the totally demolished guesten hall, the latter 'through want of care and the other through too much of it.' This was a harsh judgement by one who did not suffer fools gladly: he must have recognised that the building had stood so long because those whose main aim was simply to preserve it had carried out piecemeal, and not always appropriate, work over the previous three and a half centuries. The original stone, like that used in the priory church, was from Highley, Alverly or Ombersley - fairly local stone. Malvern's own stone was probably thought unsuitable because of the difficulty of cutting and dressing it smoothly. At various times stone was also brought from Cradley, Tisbury and Bath, and, as noted above, bricks were added to the south face. So even before 1891 the building was not very pure in the style or material of any age, and the 1891 restoration had the virtue of emphasising its late medieval character.

By this time we have more idea of the uses to which the gatehouse was put. In the mid-19th century the upper floor was used as Malvern Police Court. The ground floor was, on the east side, a store place for documents, while a fruit and game shop occupied the west side. In the early 20th century an old man recalled that in his younger days it was 'disfigured by a host of tin cats of all colours made for the purpose of scaring birds and on sale by the tenant of the Gateway who raised vegetables on the adjoining garden.' In the late 19th century the gatehouse was used as offices by solicitors and eventually by architects and estate agents. One of these was Arthur Troyte Griffith, architect friend of Sir Edward Elgar, who named the 7th Enigma Variation 'Troyte' in his honour. In 1940 Griffith wrote a paper on the gateway and read it to the Malvern Field Club. This paper has been of great use in compiling this booklet and may be consulted in the reference room of Malvern Library by anyone wanting more detailed architectural comment.

The crumbling north side before the controversial changes in 1891

Later in the 20th century the gatehouse came to be used as staff accommodation by the neighbouring Abbey Hotel. Traffic was allowed to pass through, theoretically obeying a speed limit of 4 miles an hour, though in practice this tended to be observed only by nervous learner drivers under the supervision of their instructors. Occasional slight traffic damage occurred but in 1979 an ice-cream van became dramatically lodged under the archway, causing structural damage. At last the authorities, recognising the threat to this important part of Malvern's heritage, prohibited all traffic through the archway. The gatehouse was subsequently given by de Vere Hotel (owners of the Abbey Hotel) to the Malvern Museum Society, which was experiencing difficulty in finding satisfactory premises to house its growing collection of exhibits. This was an extremely generous gift, but has left the museum with responsibility for maintaining one of the most valuable and historic buildings in Malvern - a very heavy financial burden for a charitable organisation run entirely by volunteers.

Taking over the gatehouse in 1980 enabled the volunteers to realise their dream of a museum of which Malvern can be proud. Since it is a scheduled ancient monument, the building cannot be altered in any way and careful planning is necessary to use its small rooms to best advantage. It is never forgotten that the building itself is the museum's finest and unique exhibit.

Inside, visitors are welcomed at the ground floor reception desk, with adjacent bookstall and sales area. Two steps lead up into the geological gallery with its varied information on the Malvern Hills, which were formed hundreds of millions of years ago in the pre-Cambrian period.

Every possible space is used effectively in the museum so it is well worth taking a good look at the area below, along and above the spiral staircase leading from the geological gallery. Exhibits are changed from time to time so precise details are not printed in this souvenir booklet but everything is carefully labelled and explained.

Upstairs, 4 small rooms, each with its own theme, are entered from the corridor, which is also a gallery of exhibits, including the timbers of the old guesten hall. Views from the upstairs windows give a good impression of the gatehouse's role in separating the village from the monastic estates to the south.

The first room concentrates on the medieval period. It features Malvern Priory and Malvern Chase, the medieval hunting ground loved by King John and administered from Hanley Castle, which had a thriving pottery industry.

Next is the Water Cure Room, telling the story of Malvern water from early days when it was thought to be rather special, through its exploitation for therapeutic purposes up to its present popularity as delightfully pure drinking water.

The Victorian Room shows how, as a result of the water cure and the arrival of the railway, Malvern was transformed into a fashionable spa with good facilities for visitors and numerous good schools. A great deal of Victorian social history is in evidence here.

More modern times are featured at the eastern end of the corridor gallery and the adjacent room, which shows the impact on the arts world of the Malvern Festival. Since the museum is also proud of the town's contribution to national history there are important exhibits on the development of the motor car - the famous Morgan is still produced here. Finally, the Staircase gallery illustrates the scientific advances including the research that was instrumental in defeating Hitler.

Bibliography and further reading

Obtainable only in reference libraries:

Griffith, A. Troyte: *The Priory Gateway, Great Malvern* (in 1940 Annual Report of Malvern Field Club)
Grindrod, Charles F.: *Malvern, What to See and Where to Go*, 1897
Hurle, Pamela & Winsor, John: *Portrait of Malvern*, Phillimore, 1985
Molyneux, Nicholas A.D.: *The Abbey Gateway*, Malvern Museum, 1980
Smith, Brian S.: *A History of Malvern*, Leicester University Press, 1964 and Alan Sutton, 1978

Prints, drawings and maps in Malvern Museum and Malvern Public Library

Currently available in bookshops:

Hurle, Pamela: *Bygone Malvern*, Phillimore, 1989
Hurle, Pamela: *The Malverns*, Phillimore, 1992
Hurle, Pamela: *Malvern Churches*, 2002
Weaver, Cora: *The Priory Gatehouse of Great Malvern*, 1993

Published by Malvern Museum

Printed by Aspect Design, 2nd edition 2003

 ISBN 0 9541520-3-4

9780954152031

hlight the 1891 changes:

int by Henry Lamb

Back - photo from early 20th century guide to the Imperial Hotel

THE VICTORIAN FERN CRAZE

SARAH WHITTINGHAM

SHIRE LIBRARY

Christine Hodgson